ROMAN BRITAIN

CONTENTS

ABOVE: *A relief from a Roman tombstone showing a blacksmith at work, from the Yorkshire Museum in York.*

RIGHT: *The head of Julius Caesar on a coin, one of the few made with his likeness during his lifetime.*

BRITAIN BEFORE THE ROMANS

At the time of the Roman invasions of 55 and 54BC Britain was still in the late Iron Age, inhabited by Celtic tribes whose ancestors had emigrated centuries before from the Danube basin. They had become the dominant race throughout Europe before Rome began her conquests beyond Italy. Although warlike and prone to fighting to expand tribal territory, the Celts were not the savage barbarians that Caesar described: they were a well-organized society with strict laws and a relatively advanced bronze and iron technology; they even had goldsmiths. Their houses were of wattle and daub with thatched roofs or, in the hill areas, dry stone. Most of the population lived in scattered, isolated farming communities. Their farmsteads, with granaries, storage pits, workshops and animal pens, were surrounded by banks with wattle fencing and a ditch to keep out intruders and marauding wild animals. The women spun, wove and dyed wool to make clothes. Personal appearances were important – they used soap, unlike the Romans – with both sexes wearing jewellery and taking great pride in their long, well-groomed hair.

ABOVE: *A relief of a Celtic horned god of war. The Celtic religion believed in a life after death, which led Caesar to remark that this possibly accounted for their recklessness in battle.*

As well as small communities, there were also large settlements and heavily defended forts where the chiefs and nobles lived with their warriors. The biggest settlements, such as Colchester, were tribal capitals covering several square miles and were entirely self-sufficient; here the people grew crops, grazed cattle, erected temples, and had cemeteries and rubbish

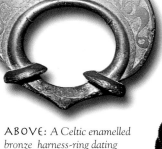

ABOVE: *A Celtic enamelled bronze harness-ring dating from the 1st century. The Celts perfected the art of enamelling, and decorated many objects using this technique. However, their distinctive style was lost after the Roman invasion.*

LEFT: *This traditional decorative gold torc, showing the sophistication of Celtic metalwork, would be worn around the neck.*

LEFT: *The Waterloo helmet, recovered from the River Thames. Helmets such as these were made from bronze and sometimes decorated with gold or silver. They were worn by Celtic warriors in battle to give them a fearsome appearance.*

ABOVE LEFT: *An intricately decorated dagger made from iron and bronze.*

LEFT: *How an Iron Age settlement might have looked. The Celts lived in close tribal communities and worked hard growing crops and tending herds of animals. Wealth was measured in size of cattle herds.*

BELOW: *The Celts were skilled potters, as well as being adept miners, smiths and tool-makers.*

is why they collected the heads of their enemies killed in battle while those captured alive became slaves.

The Celts were warriors who gloried in fighting, but in battle every man strove for his own personal glory which made for a brave and fearsome rabble rather than a disciplined fighting force. Their weapons were highly decorated, but they wore little armour, often choosing to paint their bodies and fight naked. Unlike the Roman army, they deployed the war chariot with great skill, much to the surprise of Caesar's army in 55BC.

tips. In the lowlands these settlements would be surrounded by defensive earthworks, but in hill country they were encircled by broad stone walls with walkways and outer defences of sharp stone palisades. Corn was part of the staple diet, and would be par-baked before being stored in pits to provide winter food; cattle were slaughtered in the autumn and the meat smoked. Plenty of beer and wine was drunk, the latter imported from Gaul.

A superstitious people, the Celts had some 400 gods who 'lived' in oak groves, rivers, lakes and other natural places. Their priests, the Druids, were the custodians of knowledge and allowed no written language, in order to guard the secrecy of their sacred rites and their position as keepers of tribal law and history. The Celts believed that the human soul had an after life and lived in the head, which

INVASION AND CONQUEST

In 61BC, when the city state of Rome ruled the whole of Italy and much of the Mediterranean seaboard, the Senate appointed General Caius Julius Caesar to be Governor of transAlpine Gaul (France). Within four years he had conquered the whole area and stood on the north coast of France gazing at the white cliffs of Dover. He knew there was mineral wealth to be won, and that the lowlands in the south produced an abundance of corn, the staple diet of the hungry legions. Furthermore he had a good political excuse to risk the adventure since fierce warriors were being sent from the British to the continental Celts to help their ongoing resistance to the Roman occupation. On the night of 25 August 55BC Caesar sailed with 10,000 men in 80 ships across the Straits of Dover. As dawn broke, Caesar's fleet saw the army of the southern tribes of Britain massed on top of precipitous cliffs and so continued east to a shallow beach (near the present Walmer Castle), tailed by the British warriors. At first his legionaries refused to leave their ships to face the enemy's chariots churning up the water between them and the shore. Finally, shamed by a lone standard-bearer jumping into the sea, they made a bloody landing. Caesar's progress inland was painfully slow as his cavalry, aboard a fleet of transports, had been dispersed in a gale. Four weeks after landing he re-embarked his army for

LEFT: *An ambitious man, Julius Caesar's two aborted invasions of Britain brought him glory in Rome and a place in the history books.*

France, determined to return the next year and gain Britain as a Roman province.

In July 54BC, with 50,000 troops and 2,000 cavalry, he landed unopposed, marched north and crossed the Thames. To achieve any degree of conquest he had to defeat the Catuvellauni, the strongest tribe in Britain. Their stronghold was betrayed by a rival tribe, the Trinovantes, and in August, Caesar overpowered them and their chief surrendered. Despite this initial victory, Caesar once again decided to return to France where the hostile Gauls were already taking advantage of the absence of the legions.

BELOW: *British Celts' use of the chariot in battle gave them a speed and manoeuvrability that came as a surprise to the Romans.*

LEFT: *Roman troopships and supply ships as shown on Trajan's Column in Rome, a copy of which can be seen in the Victoria and Albert Museum in London.*

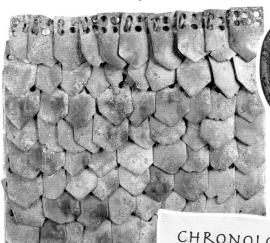

ABOVE: *Claudius, Emperor of Rome from 41 to 54AD, left Britain for Gaul only 16 days after taking Colchester.*

ABOVE: *The invading Roman army of 43AD was led by Aulus Plautius who was ordered by Emperor Claudius to 'conquer the rest of Britannia'.*

ABOVE RIGHT: *Overlapping scales of metal from Roman armour designed to protect the torso, on view at the Museum of Antiquities in Newcastle-upon-Tyne.*

The next invasion, which was to lead to 365 years of Roman rule, was ordered by Emperor Claudius in 43AD. Four legions, numbering some 24,000 men and an equal number of auxiliaries under the command of Aulus Plautius, landed in the natural harbour at Richborough on the east Kent coast. A battle on the banks of the Medway lasted two days before the Britons retreated north of the Thames, but the Romans soon crossed the river and prepared for an assault on the tribal capital of Camulodunum (Colchester). The capital was taken, and the Emperor Claudius himself made a triumphal entry at the head of his troops, riding on an elephant.

It was to take another 90 years before the whole of England and Wales was fully pacified, with Hadrian's Wall forming the northern frontier of the empire. Scotland was never subdued, nor did the Romans land in force on Irish soil.

CHRONOLOGY OF CONQUEST

43AD Emperor Claudius's army lands and takes the main tribal centre at Colchester. South-east Britain is subdued.

44–60AD Invading army divided: the II Legion goes south west where Vespasian sacks the giant Celtic hill fort of Maiden Castle in Dorset; the IX Legion goes towards Lincoln, the XIV and part of the XX into the midlands. The rest of the XX remains in reserve at Colchester.

51AD The Welsh tribes led by Caractacus are beaten in battle. He flees to north Britain where the Queen of the Brigantes betrays him to the Romans.

60AD Massacre of the Druids on Anglesey by Suetonius Paulinus, Governor of Britain.

60–61AD Boudicca, Queen of the Iceni in East Anglia, leads a revolt against the Romans and sacks Colchester, London and St Albans before she is defeated by Suetonius and commits suicide.

71–74AD The campaign against the Brigantes in the north ends with their last stand near Scotch Corner.

74–78AD Legionary fortresses established at Caerleon and Chester leading to the final subjugation of the Welsh. A legionary fortress is established at York.

83–105AD Campaigns in Scotland as far north as the Spey, but legions finally withdraw and establish the frontier of the empire on the Stanegate road across the Tyne-Solway isthmus.

122AD Hadrian arrives in Britain and work begins on his Wall.

THE ROMAN ARMY IN BRITAIN

At the time of its invasion of Britain, the Roman army was the most disciplined and efficient killing machine that the ancient world had ever known, and would remain so for the best part of 400 years. The core of this army was the infantry legion, well-armed, well-armoured and Roman citizens to a man, who served when and where needed in all parts of the empire. They formed the expeditionary force that initially conquered territories and then garrisoned forts in those occupied areas, acting as strategic reserves and tactical flying columns against incursions and insurrections. They were also skilled in civil engineering and building.

A centurion commanded 80 men divided into ten sections of eight who, when in the field, would live in goatskin tents. Six centuries of 80 men formed a cohort, and ten cohorts made up a legion with a fighting complement of about 5,000 infantry and 120 cavalry troopers as scouts, orderlies and despatch riders. The legions were supported by auxiliary infantry and cavalry units who were recruited from the natives of the Roman provinces and from border tribes. Although they were appreciated for their indigenous skills, it was the auxiliaries who were sent to the forefront in battle, being considered more expendable than the citizen legionaries who represented a much greater investment. A legion, together with its attached auxiliary units, was commanded by a senator, and under him were young military tribunes, all on short-service commissions before taking up public office. All other soldiers had to serve for 25 years, at the end of which time they received a grant of land or financial gratuity, and the auxiliaries were granted Roman citizenship. They would almost certainly stay on in a civilian settlement or town, plying a trade learned in the army.

RIGHT: A roof tile from Holt in Clwyd showing the charging wild boar emblem of the XX Legion 'Valeria Victrix' who were stationed at Chester.

BELOW: A Roman belt buckle found at Mucking, Essex, worn by soldiers and government officials.

The centurions maintained discipline and enforced rigorous and continuous combat training. During four months of initial training, recruits were loaded with heavy backpacks and did two sessions of weapon training a day with heavily weighted weapons to develop muscle. They also practised hand-to-hand

LEFT: The testudo, or tortoise, a Roman tactic of linking shields to give protection against enemy missiles. Roman soldiers were able to pile up earth against the lowest part of a Celtic hill fort under cover of the testudo and then breach the defences with relative ease.

combat with javelin and sword tips covered. Forced marches of 20 or 30 miles were common, and building practice camps honed their skills in tree-felling, timber-cutting and making ditches and ramparts. Siege warfare was practised against abandoned hill forts. Every legionary also had to be able to swim and cook and have basic building and civil engineering skills. In addition to his weapons, each legionary carried the tools needed to build defences – spade, pickaxe, saw and basket for moving earth.

There were many specialist craftsmen in a legion, such as the master builder, the surveyor, catapult maker, arrow maker and boat builder, as well as regimental priests or soothsayers. Finally there were the medical officers, usually Greek, and medical orderlies. The highly trained and valuable Roman soldier could always expect the best possible medical attention.

RIGHT: *A ballista, or huge crossbow, was part of the Roman artillery, firing stones or javelins. The strongest could hurl a javelin 1,000 yards (915m), over twice as far as the famous English longbow of the Middle Ages.*

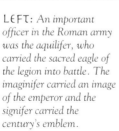

LEFT: *An important officer in the Roman army was the aquilifer, who carried the sacred eagle of the legion into battle. The imaginifer carried an image of the emperor and the signifer carried the century's emblem.*

RIGHT: *Roman medical instruments. Surgery, mostly amputation, was carried out with some skill, albeit without anaesthetic other than copious draughts of wine.*

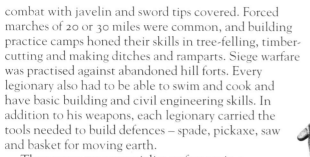

VIII
CAMPS AND FORTS

Wherever a Roman army on the march stopped for the night it surrounded its camp with a ditch and earthworks topped by a palisade of pointed poles which the troops carried as part of their equipment. It is remarkable that in a few hours legionaries were able to build ramparts and ditches around camps covering 30 to 100 acres (12 to 40ha). Legionary fortresses averaged about 50 acres (20ha) and were laid out with rounded corners in the shape of a playing card. In the beginning they had turf ramparts and timber buildings, but were later rebuilt in stone. Caerleon in South Wales, Chester and York were the three permanent legionary bases.

ABOVE: *The imposing west gate, reconstructed at Roman Fort Museum in South Shields, Tyne and Wear.*

In the centre of a fort was the headquarters building with a hall capable of holding the whole legion. It also contained administrative offices, a strong room and a shrine to the emperor where the standards were kept. The commander's house was built around a courtyard with its own bath house. Within the fort were granaries, workshops and rows of barrack blocks each holding 80 men. The whole was surrounded by high castellated walls with a walkway for the guard and turrets at regular intervals. Being a fire hazard, because of the wood-burning furnaces, the garrison bath house was always built outside the walls. Forts on a similar pattern but covering no more than 5 acres (2ha), such as those on Hadrian's Wall, were the bases for auxiliary units, and fortlets holding detachments of up to 100 men were interspersed between the bigger forts.

ABOVE: *A detachment of Legio VIII Augusta at Milecastle 49 on Hadrian's Wall. The wall was maintained by legionaries but manned by auxiliaries, and each of the 79 milecastles provided living space for a few men.*

BELOW: *Hardknott Castle (Mediobogdum), an auxiliary fort sitting high in the hills in the Lake District, was built at the beginning of the 2nd century during Hadrian's reign and, to the east, has an imposing parade ground.*

ROADS

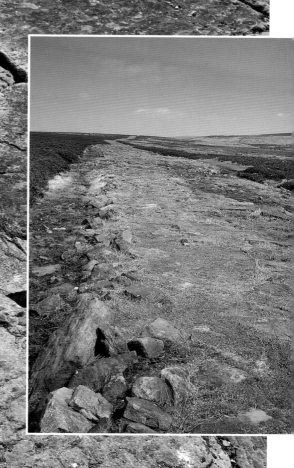

The majority of the known 8,000 miles (13,000km) of Roman roads in Britain were built during the latter half of the 1st century, following closely behind the advancing Roman army, to provide fast movement of men, materials and despatches. Initially, roads linked military camps and forts that were established approximately 15 miles (24km) apart, the regulation distance for a day's march. Later more were built to link towns.

The first road (Watling Street) ran from Richborough to Wroxeter, then west to Wales and north to Chester. Ermine Street was the main road from London northwards, while the straightest of all their straight roads was Fosse Way from Ilchester, through Bath, thence across country to join Ermine Street at Lincoln.

Wherever possible Roman surveyors made their alignments from one high point to another, but they were not averse to making a deviation in order to avoid very steep ground or marsh or to reach a suitable place to ford a river. Cuttings were made through the tops of hills, and gradients of more than one in six were crossed by cutting zig-zag terraces.

Road building was carried out by legionaries and conscripted native gangs of labourers. Using local materials, the standard technique was to dig a drainage ditch either side of a route and pile the spoil up in between to form an embankment, known as an agger. On that were laid large stones, sometimes with a kerb, then a layer of smaller stones and gravel rammed hard to consolidate and form a camber for drainage. All roads were marked by engraved or painted milestones, and posting houses were built along the main routes for the imperial postal service and official travellers.

TOP RIGHT: *Roman carts were usually built with wheels 4 feet 8 inches (143cm) apart and this became a standard gauge once ruts had been worn in the roads. It led eventually to the gauge used on many railway systems, as steam-engines first pulled carts in mines once worked by the Romans.*

RIGHT: *The Roman road at Wheeldale, North Yorkshire. Roads varied in width from 20 to 30 feet (6 to 9m) depending on their importance, although very few were paved like those in Rome.*

TOWNS AND URBANIZATION

The Roman culture was an urban one, and the legions had the twin tasks of first subduing conquered territories and then encouraging the Romanization and urbanization of the tribal nobility by allowing them to run their own affairs and enjoy a Roman standard of living. There was no town planning in Britain before the Romans came, but within six years of the Claudian invasion Colchester was founded in 49AD around a legionary fort, itself on the site of the Trinovantian capital. It was a chartered colonia, a town largely reserved for army veterans. It had the status of municipium as,

RIGHT: A reconstruction drawing of Wroxeter showing on the right the forum, with its covered walkway containing shops and offices on three sides and basilica on the fourth.

was good Roman money to be made from the relatively well-off soldiery. These became vicus with permanent homes and shops under military supervision.

Romano-British towns were laid out with streets in a grid pattern. The town centre was dominated by the forum, a large colonnaded courtyard which served as a market place and assembly ground for public gatherings. On one side was the basilica where the tribunes sat and dispensed justice. In the absence of prisons, punishment was by fine, confiscation, flogging, hard labour in mines and quarries, or execution. Every town had a mansio, the Roman equivalent of a coaching inn. Social life centred on the town bath house, a large and grand edifice. Streets were surfaced with limestone and

ABOVE AND RIGHT: *Silchester enclosed by its city walls as it may have appeared in Roman times. Having selected and planned a site, and provided some aid in building a town and setting up an administrative system, the Romans left the locals to run it.*

FAR RIGHT INSET: *Detail from a 2nd-century mosaic pavement in Winchester City Museum.*

in due course, did London, Lincoln, Gloucester and York. These towns were self-governing: everyone had to abide by Roman law, with magistrates and councils modelled on the municipal system in Rome.

In lesser towns, or civitas, a degree of tribal law and organization was maintained with magistrates elected from the native plutocracy. Many small towns began as the squatter camps of traders and camp followers outside the walls of a fort, where there

TOWNS AND URBANIZATION

gravel which would be added to as need demanded. The public water supply came via contour aqueducts or clay pipes from distant springs or reservoirs to be distributed by lead or wooden pipes. The bigger towns had stone-lined underground sewers fed by timber-lined drains from individual buildings.

The noble and wealthy among the British tribes soon acquired a taste for the Roman lifestyle and built themselves fine town houses with under-floor heating in the main rooms. Most people lived in colonnaded terraces of simple wooden houses. Many were craftsmen or shopkeepers trading from their own front rooms which would be open to the street so that they could display their goods. As they accumulated money and rose up the social ladder, they formed a new middle class alongside functionaries and professionals. In time, they also built their own town houses with rooms round a courtyard or garden which afforded privacy and dampened street noises. Mosaic floors were laid in house and courtyard, and the plaster walls decorated with religious or pastoral motifs.

BELOW: A reconstruction of a 1st-century Roman dining-room in the Museum of London using objects discovered on sites in the city. Household items were imported at first, until gradually they began to be made locally.

LONDON (LONDINIUM)

The walls of Roman London enclosed an area of 330 acres (132ha), making it the fourth largest city north of the Alps. It was the political, financial and commercial centre of Britain and its capital. Colchester was certainly the original capital, being the first town to be set up by the Romans. But London, with its busy port giving direct access to the sea and as the hub of the country's road system, became the commercial centre and *de facto* capital when Julius Agricola became governor of Britain and built his great palace on the site of what is now Cannon Street Station. Trade into the port of London was dominated by imported pottery, particularly the glossy red Samian ware that was fashionable in thousands of Romano-British homes. Wine from Gaul, Spain, Greece and Italy came a close second. Many seagoing cargo ships were fitted out to carry hundreds of fragile amphora, with space given to glassware, both utility and decorative, from Italy and Gaul. From London, barges took cargoes inland up the Thames or round the coast. Most delicacies, especially olive oil, were imported, although Britain returned the compliment with oysters, and also exported woollen cloaks together with corn, iron, copper, tin, silver and even gold. The tidal reaches of rivers extended further inland than they do today, and York and Chester were also busy seaports.

ABOVE: The pharos or lighthouse, which was built by the Romans at Dover to guide the merchant ships across the Channel, can be seen in the grounds of Dover Castle.

ABOVE: *Roman coins made from gold, silver, bronze and copper were given a fixed value by Emperor Augustus (27BC–14AD). They were used throughout the empire and encouraged trade to flourish.*

RIGHT: *The courtyard garden of a Roman town house (domus) at the Corinium Museum in Cirencester.*

Furniture was sparse and functional, and a shrine would be erected to a household god. Gardens were formal with ponds and fountains, but included beds for herbs, fruit and vegetables; the Romans introduced hundreds of plant species into Britain.

Slaves were numerous and some even became part of the family, running businesses for their masters, while others gained high places in the civil service or local administration. This enabled them to build up suffi-cient wealth from perks to buy their freedom, or they might be rewarded with it as a gift from their masters.

For all their grand buildings, Romano-British towns were small compared with those of today. London, the biggest, was no larger than the present City of London's square mile while Caistor was a mere 540 square yards (450sq m). Yet they were not so small considering that the population of Britain during the Roman occupation was only about two million – less than a quarter of the population of London today.

BATH (AQUAE SULIS)

Unlike all other Romano-British towns, Bath existed solely as a spa and, except for London, was the most cosmopolitan town in the country. From the thermal spring flowed the sacred water of the Celtic spirit Sulis, whom the Romans identified with Minerva, the goddess of healing. They built a temple to Sulis-Minerva and channelled the spring water into a huge lead-lined bath. Round this they built a full-scale bath complex and exercise hall. The temple, unlike other Celtic-Romano ones, was a full-scale classical building with a magnificent head of Medusa sculpted in the likeness of a barbarian Celt. The temple became the centre of a cult to Minerva with its own priest, the only such one in Britain, who interpreted omens and prepared sacrificial victims. Both the temple and the baths were visited by people from all over Europe, particularly those seeking cures.

ABOVE: *According to Hadrian (Emperor 117–138AD), the wall was to separate the barbarians from the Romans and allow the occupation to be consolidated in peace.*

BELOW: *Housesteads, added after the wall was finished, is one of 16 forts on Hadrian's Wall.*

RIGHT INSET: *Remains of the granary in the centre of Housesteads Fort. The stone pillars supported the floor and allowed hot air to move round underneath to dry the grain.*

Standing on a high point of Hadrian's Wall, buffeted by a keen Northumbrian wind and looking out over the wide-open, sparsely inhabited landscape to an horizon cloaked in mist, the Roman soldier from a far-off corner of the empire must have thought that there to the north were not only barbarians but, surely, the ends of the earth. Following the Claudian invasion of 43AD, it took another 60 years before the country was pacified as far north as a chain of forts along the Stanegate, a military road running east–west across the Tyne–Solway isthmus to form a border that remained disputed, undefined and under almost continual attack until Emperor Hadrian visited Britain in 122AD. He decided on a policy of damage limitation and ordered a wall to be built across England from the Tyne estuary to the Solway Firth, a distance of 73 miles (117km) or 79 Roman miles.

Hadrian's Wall was built not by slave labour but by legionaries, the élite troops of the Roman army who were as skilled in civil engineering as they were in fighting. It was a massive engineering feat requiring immense manpower, finance and logistic support. It was to be built of stone 10ft (3m) wide and 15ft (5m) high with a protective ditch, like a tank trap, 13ft 6in (4m) deep in front of it. The garrison would be stationed in castles set at one-mile (1.6km) intervals along it, and in turrets or signal towers in between. Infantry and cavalry forts just behind or astride the wall would reinforce and relieve the garrisons. Behind the wall a fossa, or ditch, 20ft (6m) wide would define the boundary of the military zone. During building, the width of much of the wall was reduced to 7ft (2m) to speed up the work, and the western end was only a turf wall with a timber palisade. The whole project, including the quarrying of 27 million cubic feet (765,000cu m) of stone, was completed in just over seven years. A force of between 11,000 and 12,000 men was needed to man its 156 turrets, 79 milecastles and 16 forts. The garrisons were auxiliaries, not legionaries, who acted as frontier police collecting tolls from the customs posts at the milecastles, as well as front-line troops taking the brunt of tribal attacks. The legions remained in their permanent forts and were used only in major campaigns, for heavy punitive expeditions or to repel invaders. In Hadrian's time there were three legions, each of about 5,000 men, stationed in Britain, the nearest to the wall being based at York some 85 miles to the south.

When the Antonine Wall was built further north between the Firth of Forth and the Clyde in 139–140AD, Hadrian's Wall was evacuated, but in 155AD the garrison returned. In the ensuing 255 years Hadrian's Wall was breached four times by the barbarians, to be rebuilt in parts from the foundations up. By 410AD the last garrison had gone and the wall became a ready source of dressed stone for farm, town, church and road building. Notwithstanding 1,600 years of pillage and decay, there are still long stretches rising and falling dramatically along the precipitous ledges of great crags and rocky sills. What remains is an impressive monument to the greatest civil engineering project undertaken in pre-modern Britain.

FARMS AND VILLAS

As towns were built all over the province, a new urban population was created which produced no food itself but needed to be fed. With urbanization came a middle class that, along with the old tribal nobility, quickly acquired a taste for Roman living standards, which included eating well. The army of legionaries and auxiliaries also needed good nourishment. For the first time, farming became a profitable occupation. The small farmer, who had produced only for his family or local community and lacked the means of disposing of any surplus, now found a road to the nearest town's granary and market hall where his produce could be sold. Aided by Roman advice on crop rotation and intensive animal breeding, he was able to increase production and grow the new vegetables and herbs introduced by the Romans. It was not long before he had abandoned his clay-and-wattle hut and built a small house.

Over the generations these simple farmhouses were added to, rebuilt and again enlarged to compare with upper-class town houses, and were furnished in Roman style. Wealthy townsmen and landowners took up farming, too, as a business investment and

BELOW: Villas, the country houses and farms belonging to wealthy townsmen and landowners, were often extended and made more luxurious during the Roman period.

RIGHT: A fragment of wall decoration dating from the 2nd century, from Fishbourne Roman palace in Sussex.

built themselves country homes with bath houses, formal gardens, courtyards, estate offices and accommodation for farm bailiffs, servants and slaves, the whole enclosed within walls. They were called villas, and by the mid-3rd century had become as grand as their counterparts in Italy. Some were veritable palaces, like Fishbourne in Sussex, which covered an area the size of Buckingham Palace. It was an exceptional building, having been started as early as 85AD, whereas most villas were built after the mid-2nd century. Some were the centre of small farms; others – for example, Bignor in Sussex – were surrounded by estates of about 3,000 acres (1,214ha).

Villas, like town houses, were lavishly decorated with marble or mosaic floors and walls of painted plaster, and the principal rooms would have under-floor heating provided by a complex hypocaust system. Daylight indoors must have been dim as window glass was a translucent green and, come dusk, oil lamps provided only a low level of light.

ABOVE: The wealthier villa owners had fine painted plaster walls and luxurious bath houses. This wall painting from the bath house at Sparsholt villa in Hampshire can be seen at Winchester City Museum.

RIGHT: *The head of Medusa, a detail from the mosaic on the floor of the heated changing room (apodyterium) in the baths complex at Bignor Roman villa, Sussex.*

RIGHT: *Part of the bath house at Chedworth villa, Gloucestershire, showing the mosaic floor of the warm room (tepidarium), the wall flues and the hypocaust pillars of the hot room (caldarium).*

The sites of about 2,000 Roman villas have been located, many from aerial photographs of crop markings. Their distribution fans out in diminishing density from the home counties to Wales, and is non-existent in Devon, Cornwall, the far north west of England and north of Yorkshire. This distribution conforms to the fertile lowland areas of Britain, where arable and mixed farming were profitable, while in the hill country and moorland area farming barely changed from pre-Roman times.

LEFT: *A detail showing a drunken satyr and maenad (reveller) from the mosaic in the dining room at Chedworth villa, Gloucestershire.*

LEISURE

The Celts had always been a clean race, but the Romans developed cleanliness to a fine art and made it one of life's pleasures. Every town had its bath complex, as did inns and all the best houses. From a changing room a person proceeded via a cold plunge through a sequence of hot, warm and cold rooms, both dry and wet. Along the way oil was rubbed over the body and allowed to seep into the pores opened by the heat. In the hottest areas the oil and body dirt were removed with a blunt curved scraper or strigil. A rinse in a warm water bath was followed by another cold plunge to close the pores again, and a massage might also be enjoyed along the way. It was an unhurried process and a social occasion with gambling and gossip while you sweated.

Public baths and those outside army forts were the Roman equivalent of modern sports centres; an outdoor swimming pool, like the one at Wroxeter, was a rare facility. Gambling was endemic in Romanized society and in the army, dice being the commonest game. Chariot racing, like horse racing today, provided another gambling venue.

Many towns boasted an amphitheatre, usually built on the outskirts. The one at the legionary fort of Chester was constructed first in wood in the late 1st century, then enlarged and replaced in stone. The amphitheatre at Caerleon in Wales, a squat oval 250ft x 200ft (76m x 61m), is the best-preserved example in Britain. Built about 90AD, it was used both for games and as a military training arena; most of its sport was cruel and grisly. Games were held on religious and military festivals and certainly on the emperor's birthday. The 'stars' of the entertainment world were the

ABOVE: *Much of the stonework at Caerleon amphitheatre is intact, buttressing the now grass-covered earthworks which supported stone terraces and wooden seating for 6,000 people.*

ABOVE: *The character types in Roman plays were often similar so actors wore masks to make the characters easily identifiable to the audience from a distance.*

RIGHT: *The baths complex in the foreground and the exercise hall beyond at Wroxeter, Shropshire.*

BELOW: *Bath houses included an exercise hall or palaestra such as this one, where some went to wrestle or weight lift, others to stroll and chat, buy snacks from vendors or gamble.*

ABOVE: The 'Colchester Vase', c.140–200AD. It shows two gladiators, the secutor on the left in full armour and the retiarius on the right with trident and net; his finger is raised in submission.

gladiators, and the best ones earned fortunes. They fought each other or, when available, prisoners-of-war or convicted criminals for whom an appearance in the ring meant almost inevitable execution. Further amusement was provided by acrobats and jugglers, wrestling, boxing with mailed fists, bear-baiting and mock hunts of wild animals, particularly

boar. The amphitheatre was an important political tool, since it was important to keep the populace in good mood.

The theatre that can still be seen at St Albans, known in Roman times as Verulamium, was built in the middle of the 2nd century. It was horseshoe-shaped, with steep tiers of seats embraced by a buttressed stone wall, and a stone stage with a back-drop of columns. Performances included plays and pantomimes, songs and recitations; possibly also religious plays.

The family played games similar to draughts and chess with pieces made of bone or pottery, and for musical entertainment there were the lyre and the cithera, a triangular instrument with seven to eleven strings which the god Aureus is seen playing in mosaics. The towns had wine shops and restaurants, and the urban Briton acquired the Latin habit of spending much leisure time eating and drinking on the pavement beneath the porticos that lined the streets. With slaves to do the work, and even manage businesses for their masters, the well-to-do had plenty of time for entertaining and the pursuit of a café society.

BELOW: A gaming-board, dice and counters found at Corbridge on Hadrian's Wall. Games like draughts might have been played with counters like these.

FASHION AND FOOD

Life changed very little for the native peasants living outside the towns and villa estates. Their houses remained simple undecorated huts, their clothes were made from home-spun wool, and they grew their own grain for the staple diet of bread and porridge. They had little if any furniture, but might own a few pieces of Celtic or Roman-style jewellery. Their Celtic customs and religious beliefs survived the Roman occupation, although they did accept some Roman deities alongside their own, and Christianity. But the Romanized and urbanized middle and upper classes lived in style and comfort, eating a wide variety of food, drinking good wines and enjoying a social life.

A man wore a simply cut tunic which also did service as a nightshirt. If he were on official business he would wear a toga over the tunic, but if not he would put on a long overtunic held in by a belt or girdle and, in cold weather, a cloak. Footwear was usually leather sandals on bare feet, or boots in cold wet weather. A lady, assisted by a servant, took great care over her appearance. She had mirrors made of polished bronze and combs of bone, and her hairstyle would be very elaborate, possibly using false pieces or wigs – anything to keep up with the latest fashion from Rome. White lead, ochre, chalk, charcoal and other materials would be ground in

RIGHT: *Jewellery found at Rhayader in Powys. The necklet is decorated with cornelians, blue paste and borders of filigree.*

oils to make cosmetic paste to be applied with glass rods and spatulas. Her ankle-length tunic would be covered by a shorter one or toga-type drapery and she wore brightly coloured sandals. The colour of a lady's dress would denote her rank, as would the jewellery she wore; a patrician, for instance, could wear a diadem on her head, while a plebeian could not.

The main meal of the day, with food selected from a wide range of meat, fruit and vegetables, was eaten in the evening. Among the upper classes dinner would be liberally washed down with wines from Italy, Spain, France and Germany, all of a far better quality than the vinegary variety that was part of a soldier's rations. The artisan drank beer brewed from barley, as did the Celtic peasant, and mead was a popular strong drink with all classes. Wealthy Romano-Britons had slaves in the kitchen who

ABOVE LEFT: *This silver bowl and lid from the Mildenhall treasure, dating from the 3rd to 4th centuries, has a decorative frieze of animals and heads in profile with a leaf pattern above. The handle is a sea god blowing through a shell-trumpet.*

LEFT: *A reconstruction of a typical Roman kitchen at Verulamium Museum, St Albans showing the storage jars and wide variety of foods, herbs and spices used.*

RIGHT: *A Roman wrist purse.*

BELOW LEFT: *Ornate plaiting and curling of the hair became fashionable for women during imperial times; this style dates from the Flavian dynasty (69–96AD).*

were supervised by the lady of the house. Cooking was by charcoal fire on a raised stone hearth, the pots standing on an iron griddle or suspended from above. Most of the utensils would be recognizable today although they were limited to iron, wood and pottery, and much use was made of herbs and spices.

Deep red Samian pottery ware was commonly used at table, replaced by silver or pewter on special occasions. Diners used spoons and knives (guests would bring their own), but no forks, so fingers were permitted in the politest society, and meals were eaten while reclining on couches at low tables. The importance of the table in Romano-British social life is evidenced in the wall paintings and elaborate mosaics with which householders decorated their dining rooms.

FIRST COURSE
Oysters, mussels, snails fattened on milk, endive and radish salad.

MAIN COURSE
Boiled ham with honey baked in pastry case, roast peacock served with a spiced sauce, roast venison, roast suckling pig, stuffed dormice, asparagus, cabbage, parsnips and turnips.

DESSERT
Plums, cherries, quinces, pomegranates, grapes, and pastry cases filled with honey, raisins, dates and nuts.
Bordeaux wine.

LEFT: *The museum at Cirencester displays a typical dinner party menu.*

PAGE BACKGROUND: *A detail from a bird design painted ceiling, dating from the 2nd century, at Veru-lamium Museum, St Albans.*

RELIGION

omans were driven by superstition and worshipped both their own and other people's deities. When they won in battle they embraced the gods of the vanquished who could be the manifestations of their own gods. Superstition and the fear of giving offence might be why they acknowledged most of the 400 Celtic gods they found in Britain and those from the East and Africa whom the auxiliaries brought with them. The civil and military authorities tolerated almost all religions provided they were not subversive, as Christianity was first considered to be because it would not accept emperor worship or any other god. The Druids were particularly hated by the military because they were thought to have incited Boudicca's insurrection and ensuing slaughter, and because they were the spiritual backbone of the fierce Celtic resistance in Wales. But as soon as their influence was destroyed by the massacre on Anglesey in 60AD, the Romans assimilated many Celtic religious beliefs.

ABOVE: *A Roman bronze figurine of Mars, god of war, from the site of the temple at Colchester.*

ABOVE: *Part of a wall painting from the Roman chapel added to Lullingstone villa in the late 4th century. The figure's arms are upraised in the usual attitude of prayer at this time.*

While Jupiter was always referred to as 'the best and greatest', the order of importance of other deities tended to change with the needs of the time or the individual. Shrines were erected, dedications were carved and sacrifices offered, but the gods were expected to return the favour. The farmer or would-be mother would make sacrifices to Serapis, the Egyptian god of fertility, and those seeking the cure of an affliction appealed to Sulis Minerva, goddess of healing and the cult deity of the Roman bath at Bath. Roman and Romanized families had shrines in their houses where they worshipped their

LEFT: *A typical Roman temple. Temples varied in size and style from the tiny and simple to the large and ornate, but they were usually square, surrounded by a roofed verandah, and covered about 18 square yards (15sq m).*

LEFT: *A bronze votive plaque, at Colchester and Essex Museum, made by Cintusmus the copper-smith identifying Silvanus, the Roman god of growth, fertility and the countryside, with the Celtic god Callirios.*

ABOVE: *The Temple of Mithras, c.3rd century, at Carrawburgh. The concrete posts represent the original wooden posts which supported the roof. The Mithraic form of temple with nave leading to a sanctuary and altar lived on as the basic form of Christian churches.*

LEFT: *A bronze figurine of Venus, goddess of love and beauty, found at St Albans. It was probably used in a household shrine or lararium, where the family prayed each day and offered small gifts of wine or food.*

and male bonding through secrecy appealed to the soldiers. In 313AD Emperor Constantine gave Christians freedom to worship and they were no longer persecuted, and in 375AD theirs became the state religion. They soon attacked the followers of Mithras and desecrated his temples and images.

Emperor worship, which started with the deification of Claudius after his death in 54AD, was more political than mystical and depended on how popular the emperor was with the government of the day. However, while he was alive, an emperor was endowed with spiritual power and everyone was expected to show devotion to him. There were good political reasons for upholding belief in his spirituality: it served as a unifying force throughout the empire, especially for the army, as it was his image that led them into battle, and it was for him that they were prepared to die. It could be argued that there was some correlation between the ending of emperor worship and the rise of Christianity, and the declining might of Rome in the latter part of the 4th century.

particular choice of deity as well as household spirits such as Vesta, goddess of the domestic hearth, and Janus, the two-faced god who was guardian of the doorway.

The legions had their own favourite gods, the most popular being Mithras, the Persian god of light. His cult excluded women and demanded absolute secrecy from his followers. Novices were subjected to painful and frightening initiation ceremonies to prove their bravery; the macho spirit

RIGHT: *This 4th-century mosaic floor picture from a villa at Hinton St Mary, Dorset, now at the British Museum, may be the earliest known depiction in Britain of Christ.*

LEFT: *A stone relief at the Corinium Museum, Cirencester showing three mother goddesses. They often carried symbols of fertility such as fruit, fish or bread.*

DECLINE AND FALL

RIGHT: *A Saxon copy of a Roman map showing the forts of the Saxon shore built at Brancaster, Burgh, Walton, Bradwell, Reculver, Richborough, Dover, Lympne, Pevensey and Portchester.*

The end of Roman rule in Britain came slowly, in pace with the death throes of the empire itself which was threatened by weak emperors and pressure on its over-extended frontiers. From the middle of the 3rd century, Saxon pirate raids on the east coast of Britain started in earnest, leading to the building of forts of the Saxon shore. Several times during the latter half of the century Britain was cut off from her Roman rulers by the revolt of would-be emperors.

In 367AD the unthinkable happened – the Scots from Ireland, the Picts from Scotland and the Saxons and Franks from across the North Sea all attacked at the same time. By then there were not enough Roman troops left in Britain to prevent it from being overrun. The indigenous population, having been forbidden to carry arms, was defenceless and so the invaders enjoyed a year-long bout of plunder, rape and murder. Many of the fine villas were destroyed, never to be rebuilt. Fortunately, the enemy was disunited and badly organized. Three generals were despatched from Rome to regain the province and the third, Theodosius, finally drove them out. There was peace for a while and modest prosperity in the towns. In 383AD another general, Maximus, seized power in Britain and took the best troops out of the province to fight for the imperial throne. Maximus was defeated in 388AD, but by the turn of the century the Germans had invaded Gaul and Britain was virtually cut off from Rome. By 410AD the last regular Roman soldier and administrator had left the country. Emperor Honorius released Britain from her allegiance and sent a message telling the Britons to defend their own towns. It was the end of Roman Britain.

LEFT: *The obverse of a gold solidus depicting General Magnus Maximus.*

MAIN PICTURE: *Burgh Castle, Norfolk. One of the shore forts built by the Romans to withstand Saxon raids in the 3rd and 4th centuries. The east wall is 650 feet (200m) long, 14 feet (4.3m) high and 11 feet (3.5m) thick.*

THE LEGACY

Roman rule had made no attempt to weld together a British nation. Tribal antagonism had originally been fostered by forming alliances with friendly tribes and massacring those that resisted. Eventually, as Britons of any position or wealth became thoroughly Romanized, the old tribal bonds and barriers weakened. Wealth remained a measure of social rank.

RIGHT: The statue of Trajan, Emperor 98–117AD, at Tower Hill, London.

On the credit side the Romans left Britain with a fine road system and navigable inland waterways which enabled cargoes to be moved inland. Drainage of the Fens created a complex system of natural rivers and canals, and much of it still exists. They introduced many species of fruit and vegetable, such as cherries, grapes, figs, mulberries and raisins, radishes, peas, broad beans and celery, which provided a more varied and healthy diet. Great tracts of land had been given over to farming, with corn becoming a major export. The mineral wealth of the country had been exploited and – the greatest change of all – 50 large walled towns had been built, most of which evolved into modern towns and cities.

The Christian church introduced by the Romans kept the Roman language and literature alive in the period following the fall of the empire and this enabled scholars, intellectuals, churchmen and scientists of the former Roman world to communicate with each other. The languages of modern Italian, Spanish, Portuguese, French and Romanian derive directly from Latin. Above all, by assimilating and preserving the best aspects from the cultures they absorbed into their empire, the Romans left behind the seeds of a great civilization, one that later bore the fruits of the Renaissance.

The spa waters at Bath continue to attract visitors as they have done for centuries.

RIGHT AND BELOW: The Roman Garden at Chester, just outside the city walls, with a 'present-day' Roman soldier explaining the workings of a hypocaust.

BATH

CANTERBURY

CHESTER

CIRENCESTER

PLACES TO VISIT

This list is by no means exhaustive but contains a selection of Roman sites to visit.

BATH (Aquae Sulis), Avon:
Parts of the temple and a full reconstruction of the whole baths complex can be seen in the Roman Baths Museum. Guided tours take about an hour.

BIGNOR, W. Sussex:
Well-maintained villa remains, mostly under cover and including fine mosaics, dating from the 2nd to 4th centuries.

BLACKSTONE EDGE, W. Yorks:
Unique section of paved Roman road over the Pennines.

BURGH CASTLE (Gariannorum), Norfolk:
Impressive remains of walls and bastions of 3rd-century Saxon shore fort.

CAERLEON (Isca), Gwent:
Permanent legionary fort dating from the 1st to 4th centuries; footings of barracks complete, and amphitheatre (best example in the country) fully excavated. Good museum. (CADW)

CAERWENT (Venta Silurum), Gwent:
Remains of 4th-century Romano-Celtic temple and town walls. (CADW)

CANTERBURY (Durovernum Cantiacorum), Kent:
The present city walls follow the course of the Roman defences. The underground Roman Museum has a hands-on section, contains remains of a house with fine mosaics and displays excavated finds including a splendid silver hoard.

CARLISLE (Luguvalium), Cumbria:
Tullie House Museum has many locally found artefacts.

CHEDWORTH, Glos:
Large 1st- to 4th-century villa remains include two bath suites and several mosaics, mostly under cover. There is a small museum. (National Trust)

CHESTER (Deva), Cheshire:
Once a legionary fortress, Chester also had one of the biggest stone-built amphitheatres with present-day remains just outside the city walls. The 'Dewa' Roman Experience brings to life the sights and smells of Roman Chester as well as showing excavations and a recreated fortress. Over 90 well-preserved tombstones are on display in the Grosvenor Museum. In the summer a Roman soldier gives guided walks.

CIRENCESTER (Corinium), Glos:
Second largest Roman town, of which four sections of wall remain and an impressive amphitheatre, now a series of grass mounds 36 feet (11m) high. The Corinium Museum houses a collection of mosaics for which the town was famous.

PLACES TO VISIT

COLCHESTER (Camulodunum), Essex:
The first Roman town to be built, still largely surrounded by its wall. Well-preserved remains include the double-arched Balkerne Gate, west wall guard room and the earliest-known Christian church in Britain. The Castle Museum has an excellent Roman archaeological collection.

CORBRIDGE (Corstopitum), Northumberland:
There is much to see of the great fort, built in the 1st century and enlarged over the years.

DORCHESTER (Durnovaria), Dorset:
The ruins of a 4th-century town house, with more than seven rooms, can be seen. Maiden Castle, the largest Iron Age hill fort in Britain, lies outside the town, and in Dorset County Museum is a skeleton with a Roman ballista bolt in its spine.

DOVER (Dubris), Kent:
The ruins of the pharos, a Roman lighthouse, stand within Dover Castle. In the town is the Painted House where some walls still stand up to 6 feet (2m) high.

FISHBOURNE, W. Sussex:
A palatial house built soon after the 43AD invasion, it covered some 10 acres (4ha). It is thought to have been the most magnificent house outside Italy.

HADRIAN'S WALL, Cumbria & Northumberland:
The most dramatic and best-preserved section is the 12 miles (19km) between Birdoswald Fort and Housesteads Fort. Further east are the important sites of the Temple of Mithras at Carrawburgh, Chesters Fort and Corbridge. (English Heritage)

HARDKNOTT FORT (Mediobogdum), Cumbria:
The ruins, mostly consolidated, are spread over a large rocky ledge near the summit of Hardknott Pass.

LINCOLN (Lindum), Lincs:
The Newport Arch; also Foss Dyke, part of the Roman inland navigation system, runs out of the yacht basin, a one-time Roman port.

LONDON (Londinium):
The recently refurbished Roman London Gallery at the Museum of London, London Wall has on display recent finds from excavations in London. Other sites include the Temple of Mithras and sections of the Roman city wall.

LULLINGSTONE, Kent:
A well-excavated Roman villa with hypocausts and mosaics. (English Heritage)

NEWCASTLE-UPON-TYNE (Pons Aelius), Tyne & Wear:
The Museum of Antiquities has a full-scale replica of the Temple of Mithras and other artefacts from Hadrian's Wall.

DORCHESTER

FISHBOURNE

LINCOLN

LONDON

PORTCHESTER

ST ALBANS

SILCHESTER

YORK

PLACES TO VISIT

PEVENSEY CASTLE (Anderida), E. Sussex:
A Saxon shore fort, its walls still stand 28 feet high (9m) on an 8-acre (3ha) site, where the Normans built a castle.

PORTCHESTER (? Portus Adurni), Hants:
A 9-acre (3.5ha) Saxon shore fort, within walls 20 feet (6m) high, built on a promontory in Portsmouth harbour. A Norman keep and an abbey shelter within the walls which are still lapped by the sea at high tides.

RICHBOROUGH (Rutupiae), Kent:
The defensive ditches of this first camp set up by the Roman invaders are still visible. Later a Saxon shore fort covered the site. Here it is possible to trace development over nearly four centuries. (English Heritage)

ROCKBOURNE, Hants:
The remains of a villa with good mosaics, bath house and small museum.

ST ALBANS (Verulamium), Herts:
Roman town, noted for the substantial remains of its theatre. Part of the town wall and the dining-room of a town house with painted walls and mosaics can be seen. Finds are displayed in Verulamium Museum.

SILCHESTER (Calleva Atrebatum), Hants:
Nearly two miles (3km) of 3rd-century town walls now surround only fields and farms. Beyond them are the remains of an amphitheatre. (English Heritage)

SOUTH SHIELDS (Arbeia), Tyne & Wear:
Good museum with a full-scale reconstruction of the fort's main gate-house.

VINDOLANDA, Hexham, Northumberland:
Roman fort on Hadrian's Wall dating from 85AD. Vindolanda is rich in archaelogical finds which are displayed in the museum. Remains include a large praetorium and many recently excavated buildings.

WINCHESTER (Venta Belgarum), Hants:
At one time the fifth largest Roman city in Britain, fragments of mosaic and wall paintings are now on display in the City Museum.

WROXETER (Viroconium Cornoviorum), Shropshire:
Only the vast bath complex has been excavated; its exercise hall is a splendid example of Roman masonry and, unusually, it has an outdoor swimming pool.

YORK (Eboracum), N. Yorks:
In 71–73AD Eboracum was built to help subdue the turbulent north, developing into a colonia with 4,000 men. The remaining Roman walls include the ten-sided Multangular Tower and the Anglian Tower. Collections in the Yorkshire Museum reflect the history.